DOVEDALE GU

C000016155

DOVEDALE has long been acknowledged as a gem of English scenery. Successive generations have delighted in its beauty, though not all have admired it for the same reasons. Early in the 19th century Dovedale Gorge, with its wooded slopes, with its tall sombre pinnacles of rock, with, all in all, its air of wild remoteness from the outer world, had a potent and intoxicating effect on romantic imaginations. Dovedale, according to the commentators, was savage: it was awful: it was sublime. It was, in short, grossly overwritten.

(opposite) Fly-fishing in the River Dove above the Stepping Stones

(below) The Dove between Thorpe Cloud and Bunster

Contem the artis medium descripti valley of fashions in scenery change and today, if we look at the illustrations in this booklet (seen through the unsentimental lens of the camera) we are inclined to go back to an earlier, pre-romantic view of Dovedale as a 'calm sequestered scene'.

There are other charming stretches above the celebrated Gorge and this guidebook describes and illustrates the eight-mile walk up the river Dove from Thorpe, through the remarkably beautiful two-mile stretch of Dovedale Gorge, on through Mill Dale, Wolfscote Dale and Beresford Dale to finish at

the attractive Derbyshire village of Hartington.

The southern entrance to Dovedale is dominated by two hills, the green, grey-capped rocky cone of Thorpe Cloud to the south-east of the river, and Bunster, with its steep inner face overlooking the valley, to the north-west. The road between Thorpe and Ilam passes in front of these hills; just beyond the bridge over which it crosses the Dove an access road leads past the entrance to the Izaak Walton Hotel and on to a public car park for visitors to Dovedale. There are other routes into the Gorge, both passing to the right of Thorpe Cloud: one path leads through the grounds of the Peveril of the Peak Hotel, a few hundred yards on the Ashbourne side of Thorpe village, and the other begins in the village itself.

Most of Dovedale is now owned by the National Trust, Britain's largest conservation charity. The dale is farmed, as are most of the surrounding hilltops and slopes, with cattle on the high ground and sheep on the rocky slopes and in the woods. However, the Trust does now fence from grazing a lot of the woodland, to assist its natural regeneration and to encourage a varied wildlife within it. Because of the farming, visitors are asked to keep strictly to the Countryside Code, particularly by keeping dogs under control, shutting all gates, and not damaging walls by climbing on them.

The spectacular sights of Dovedale Gorge lie within a few minutes walk of Thorpe. But the energetic may prefer, before going up the dale, to climb Thorpe Cloud. (For the sake of preserving the hillside, please follow your own route to the top). Dovedale is for the connoisseurs not only of valley scenery, but of hill-top views as well. It is, on a windy day, a blustery

(opposite) Thorpe Cloud and the Stepping Stones

(below) The Stepping Stones

(above) View upstream above the Stepping Stones

(opposite) Bunster viewed from Thorpe Cloud

scramble up the springy grass slopes, close-cropped by the sheep. But the long views from the top repay the effort. Immediately below, as one stands on the ridge at the top of Thorpe Cloud, is the village; a grey-stone village, set pleasantly on green hillocks. To the south stretches a rolling landscape of wood and field, the fields mostly pasture now, though just below, around Thorpe, the long ridges in the grass indicate the strip holdings of a medieval open-field arable system. Looking to the high ground to the north the aspect is altogether different. The wooded upper slopes of the Gorge twist away towards more hills, misty green in the distance. The Gorge is flanked by upland fields. Not here the rich hedged meadows of the lower land, but instead

bleaker grey-green sheep pastures, intersected by limestone walls. The Dove itself is invisible, save where it flows sparkling out of the Gorge, and where occasional glimpses of it can be caught as it winds its way across the lower ground southward. The whole panorama is exhilarating, as long views from heights always are.

The National Trust restricts access along Dovedale to the eastern or Derbyshire side. This policy in fact benefits visitors, giving them a quiet bank to look at, and also helping to preserve wildlife.

In the leisurely days of the 19th century it was fashionable to proceed up Dovedale (silk-hatted and sedate) upon the back of a donkey: we now take our pleasures more freely and energetically.

Walking then, we follow the limestone path beyond the Stepping Stones, across a flat stretch of riverside grass once inelegantly known as the Sow-Sitch. Already, with Thorpe Cloud blocking the backward view, we have the feeling of being shut in.

The most curious features of the Dovedale scene are its rock formations, incidental products of that geological process which has, through immemorial time, fashioned the main shape of the Gorge itself. Many of the rocks in the area used to be parts of active coral reefs. More recently, flowing water, aided by the wind and the rain, has eaten away the softer limestone. In some places caverns or arches have been formed. In others, where the harder rock has offered greater resistance to the erosion, huge crags or pinnacles have been left projecting from the sides of the valley. Lichens cover parts of some of them; but for the most part they stand out bare, grey and massive. Many of them have been named, with more or less free historical imagination.

The first of them, Dovedale Castle, is to be seen opposite a slight rise in the path beyond the Sow-Sitch. Upstream of the Castle, again on the Staffordshire side, is a whole group of rocks, the Twelve Apostles, St. Peter foremost. Here as elsewhere, the National Trust periodically carries out tree and scrub clearance to make the rock formations more visible. About here we begin to enter the most characteristic and lovely part of the Gorge. Its walls rise high, 400 to 500 feet above the river. It is amusing, incidentally, to note a change in verbal fashions. It is quite impossible for us, though it was common in the nineteenth century, to talk of Dovedale's 'mountains'. We expect – vulgarly no doubt – something rather larger of our mountains. But this – mere size not being all – is no disparagement of the glories which

(opposite) Tissington Spires

(below) The Twelve Apostles

may legitimately be claimed for Dovedale. It is a valley of rich green. The Derbyshire side is overgrown with hazel and ash trees, and the Staffordshire side even more thickly wooded; the foliage ascends, bank upon bank, in billows of green, to the top of the valley, softening the hard outline of the rock. Dovedale's woods are a great part of its glory: they are the background to every scene in the Gorge, the dark setting against which the buttresses and needles of rock are displayed. The woods have great botanical as well as scenic interest: they are predominantly ashwood, together with beech, sycamore and conifers that have been planted at various times either for scenic or commercial purposes. Even-aged stands of young ash indicate areas which have been grazed comparatively recently.

The river flows, quick and clear, between tree-shaded banks, over a succession of small weirs. Trout and grayling play in its shallow

(above) Dovedale Church

(opposite) The impressive arch in front of Reynard's Cave

waters. At few points can more than a short stretch of the river be seen. It is too sinuous, and its windings are too closely followed by the valley walls, for extensive views to be possible. As one looks up the Gorge its sides seem to meet one another in green interlocking folds. Opposite the Twelve Apostles is Lover's Leap. The melancholy tale is told of a young woman who, for unrequited love, cast herself over the precipice, only to be saved from death by the bushes which broke her fall. She lived soberly and singly, and it is to be trusted not too unhappily, ever after.

Beyond Lover's Leap the path descends to another group of rocks, the Tissington Spires, on the near side of the river. A little further

upstream on the opposite bank is a large mass of rifted rocks, indented with deep cavities and fissures known as Dovedale Church. Beyond this on the near side is Reynard's Cave, a limestone cavern with an entrance above 30 feet high and 15 feet wide. The cave is part way up the side of the valley. The entrance of the cave (of which the interior is not in itself very remarkable) is reached beyond an impressive high natural arch, with a narrow crevice in its top and a bush growing hardily within the crevice. To the left of the cave is a smaller one, Reynard's Kitchen.

Reynard's Cave has a melancholy association (better attested than the lover's leap). It was after picnicking near here, in July 1761, that Dr. Langton, Dean of Clogher in County Tyrone, was fatally injured. On horseback and with a young lady of his party riding behind, he tried to climb the steep slope towards Tissington. The ascent was too precipitous and the over-burdened horse fell, throwing both its riders. The lady recovered from her injuries; the Dean died. As the contemporary chroniclers pointed out, with gloomy relish, he had preached at All Saints', Derby, only the Sunday before, on the strangely prophetic text, 'It is appointed unto men once to die'.

Beyond Reynard's Cave the valley narrows to the Straits. There is barely room for the path beside the river, and on the Staffordshire side the rock rises sheer from the bed of the stream.

On the other side of the Straits a massive crag, the Lion's Head, projects over the path. Its resemblance to the profile of a lion is indeed remarkable, but perhaps best seen from the far side. It is incidentally, wise to be continually turning round, in Dovedale, to take a backward

(opposite) The Lion's Head Rock

(below) The Straits

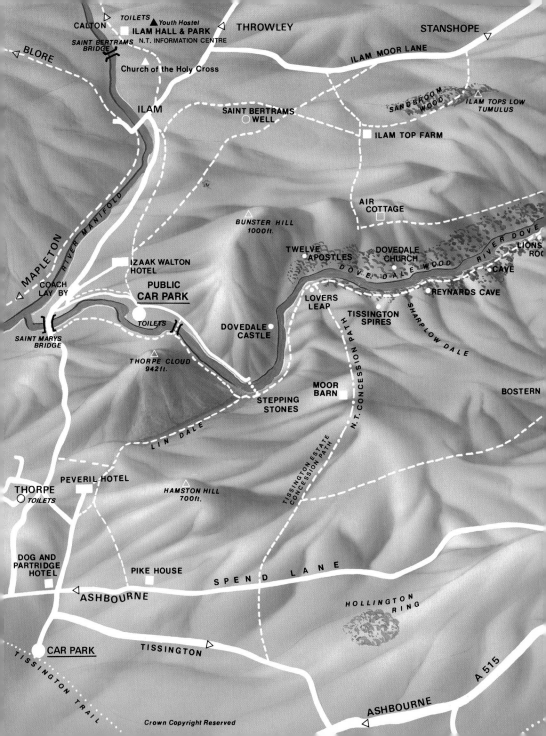

DOVEDALE

WETTON

HOPE

HOPE   HULME END

ALSTONEFIELD
TOILETS

Saint Peter's
Church

GRATTON HILL

1000 ft.

STANSHOPE
PASTURE

TOILETS
N.T. INFORMATION CENTRE

MILLDALE

VIATOR
BRIDGE

RAVENS
TOR

HURTS WOOD

HALL DALE

ICKERING
TOR

DOVE
HOLES

THE NABS

BALEY HILL
1000 ft.

SHINING
TOR

LODE
MILL

FISHPOND
PLANTATION

WOLFSCOTE DALE
BERESFORD DALE

HARTINGTON

Iron
Tors

COLDEATON

KERING DALE

NABS

DALE

0 ft.

HANSON GRANGE

THE PINCH

N.T. CONCESSION PATH

NEW
HANSON
GRANGE

MOAT LOW
TUMULUS

MOATLOW
FARM

NEW
INNS

CAR PARK

ALSOP-en-le-DALE

BUXTON

A 515

NORTH

FOOTPATHS

TISSINGTON TRAIL

PARWICH

Scale

0   1/4 Mile   1/2

(above) The Shepherd's Abbey Rocks

(opposite) Footbridge by Pickering Tors

view of the path. Unexpected beauties have a trick of revealing themselves in the shifting play of light and shade on the rocky wooded slopes.

High on the bank above the Lion's Head is a much smaller block, the Watch Tower, which has every appearance of being about to slither down into the river.

Farther upstream are the great blocks of Pickering Tors on the Derbyshire bank, and, across the river a single lichen-grown monolith, rising tall, sheer and slightly tilted; this is the famous Ilam Rock.

Near the Rock there is a footbridge, which should be crossed by those who wish to explore Hurts Wood and Hall Dale on the Staffordshire side of the river.

Hall Dale, a side valley, winds its way up to the left to the hamlet of Stanshope. Hurts Wood, which covers its southern side, is the last of the Gorge's thickly-wooded areas. The northern slope of Hall Dale, known as The Greek Temple, is comparatively bare, resembling the grass-covered, lightly-wooded slopes at the beginning of the Gorge.

Opposite Hall Dale the main footpath rises again for a little way and then descends to the Dove Holes, two large shallow caves, the last of the show-pieces of Dovedale Gorge. The larger of the two is some 50 to 60 feet wide, and 30 feet high.

Beyond the Dove Holes the main dale becomes more open. There are still, however, singular rock formations to be seen. Opposite the Holes is the Shepherd's Abbey; the name is perhaps best justified if one views the rock from a short way up the Nabs. A little farther on is Raven's Tor, a great buttress rising sheer above the Staffordshire bank. But here there is no foliage to set off the rock. Grass and gorse have replaced the trees. The mark of man is perceptible, too. Dry-stone walls intersect the grassy slopes.

The Dovedale scene, as the hamlet of Milldale is approached, becomes more domesticated still, with cows stolidly ruminating by the riverside. At Milldale the path crosses a little twin-arched bridge, the Viator Bridge mentioned by Cotton in *The Compleat Angler*. Milldale Barn, adjacent to the bridge, is now a National Trust Information Point.

A number of routes lead away from Milldale. To the left a road runs over, by way of Hopedale and Wetton, to Thor's Cave and the Manifold Valley. Half-left a track climbs up to the hill village of Alstonefield, where, in the church, the pew used by Charles Cotton may be seen. To the right there are more footpaths back over the hills to Hanson Grange and to Alsop. Straight on, the road runs along the riverside for half a mile.

At Lode Mill, river and road part company again. The road to Alsop goes off to the right, with Shining Tor on one side and the heavily-wooded slopes of Pinch Wood on the other.

The riverside path, now on the Derbyshire bank again, continues towards Wolfscote Dale and Beresford Dale. The valley opens out. Trees are sparse. The slopes provide pasture but they are still broken, here and there, by projecting crags of bare grey rock, or steep screes, too stony to allow even grass to take root.

From the east, two narrow dales come down into the valley: the first beneath the conifer-grown slopes of the Iron Tors; and the second,

(opposite) Nabs Dale

(below) The Dove Holes

Biggin Dale, three-quarters of a mile farther on, beneath the screes of Peaseland Rocks.

Beyond this point we are in Wolfscote Dale. Gratton Hill rises, 1,194 feet high, to the left, Wolfscote Hill even higher, to 1,272 feet, on the right. The scene is diversified by long screes and by pinnacles of rock.

At the far end of Gratton Hill beyond Alstonefield Bridge, the ground falls sharply and rather unexpectedly away. Round the foot of the hill the Dove receives a tributary, albeit a meagre stream. And for the first time since leaving Thorpe it is possible to stand on the river bank and look across the typical hedges and fields of the English countryside. Up to this point the valley walls have blocked all side views.

(opposite) Raven's Tor Rock

(below) Riverside path by the Nabs

From the foot of Wolfscote Hill on the right the path leads over a meadow to another footbridge and the entrance to Beresford Dale. Beresford Lane, which comes down to the river at this point, gives access to the high ground between the Dove and Manifold valleys. Branching off from it, a path goes behind Gratton Hill to Narrowdale, of which it was once picturesquely observed that it was so narrow 'that the inhabitants there, for that quarter of the year when the sun is nearest the Tropic of Capricorn, never see its face at all; and that at length, when it does begin to appear, they never see it till about one o'clock, which they call the Narrow-dale noon'.

Beresford Dale itself is forever to be associated with Izaak Walton, Charles Cotton, and that leisurely and altogether agreeable seventeenth-century classic, *The Compleat Angler, or the Contemplative Man's Recreation. Being a Discourse of Fish and Fishing, not*

19

(above) General view of Milldale

(opposite) The Viator Bridge over the Dove at Milldale

unworthy of the perusal of most Anglers.

The whole of Dovedale is, indeed, amply provided with those Literary Associations without which no beauty spot can feel itself fully equipped. This is perhaps the place to say a word about them. Michael Drayton, who in his long poem *Polyolbion*, published in 1613, conscientiously recorded the topography of England and Wales, omitted neither Dove nor Manifold from his catalogue. However, passing lightly over Walton and Cotton for the moment, it was not until the eighteenth century, when the appreciation of scenery first really developed among the English, that Dovedale became thoroughly fashionable. Johnson, to whom the Dove and Manifold are said to have suggested the setting for his allegory *Rasselas*, declared that 'he who has seen Dovedale need not travel to the Highlands'. Rousseau – a curiously appropriate admirer of Dovedale during its romantic period – visited it during his stay at Wootton Hall, near Ellastone in Staffordshire. Rather later, Byron (ranging farther afield for his testimonial than Johnson had done) wrote to Tom Moore: 'Was you ever in Dovedale? I assure you there are things in Derbyshire as noble as in Greece or Switzerland'. For Ruskin, north Derbyshire, and the Dove valley in particular, were 'an alluring first lesson in all that is admirable and beautiful'. But all these handsome tributes were those, so to say, of distinguished visitors who left kind words in the visitors' book. Tennyson, indeed, literally signed the visitors' book: he did so at the Izaak Walton Hotel, recording his opinion that Dovedale was 'one of the most unique

21

and delicious places in England'.

With Cotton and Walton, however, the associations are altogether more intimate. Beresford Hall, which stood above the Dale, was Cotton's birthplace and home. The estate had been in the hands of his mother's family, the Beresfords, since Norman times. The Hall in Cotton's day was a plain stone Tudor building, serviceable rather than ornate. Among Cotton's talents was one for horticulture, and he replanted the gardens in excellent taste. But like his father, he was chronically short of money, for he had no profession and his writings brought him no fortune; and so after twice obtaining powers from Parliament to sell part of his estates to pay his debts, he was obliged, in 1681, to dispose of the Hall itself. It subsequently passed through various changes of ownership; eventually, like others of the halls and manor-houses of the district, it lost status and became a simple farm-house. It is now in ruins.

However, the celebrated Fishing Temple, a secular shrine for all anglers, still stands, in a corner of the grounds by the river. Cotton built it in 1674, a stone single-roomed building, with his own monogram entwined with Walton's over the door. The interior was wainscoted, and had paintings of angling subjects on the larger panels. In the right-hand corner was a buffet, with folding doors, on which were portraits of Cotton, Walton and a boy-servant.

The Fishing Temple is a memorial to a noble friendship. The literary memorial to that friendship is, of course, *The Compleat Angler* itself. It was first brought out, by Walton alone, in 1653; to the 5th edition, in 1676, Cotton

(opposite) Footbridge at the end of Wolfscote Dale

(below) Wolfscote Dale

added a second part, on fly-fishing, prefixing it with an epistle, dated from Beresford, 'To my most worthy father and friend, Mr. Izaak Walton the elder'.

Beresford Dale is narrow and leafy, a charming miniature of Dovedale Gorge. Half-way along it is Pike Pool, so called, as Cotton himself tells us, because of the grey monolith, or pike, which rises out of its still waters. The Tower which stands above the Dale in the grounds of the Old Hall, the cave in which Cotton is reputed to have hidden from duns, and the Fishing Temple itself, are all in private grounds and inaccessible to the public. However, the Temple may be seen across the river from the footpath.

Beyond Beresford Dale the path leaves the river and crosses the fields into nearby Hartington, which it enters near the Charles Cotton Hotel (as those beginning their walk at Hartington may care to know).

(above) Footbridge in Beresford Dale

(opposite) Lode Mill Cottages

(back cover) The footbridge in Wolfscote Dale

Published by
DERBYSHIRE COUNTRYSIDE LIMITED
Heritage House, Lodge Lane, Derby, DE1 3HE

The text was written by Keith Mantell

Photography by Andy Williams assisted by Miss Susan Beaton Bramwell, Brian Lawrence, Gary Wallis, Roy Deeley, Studio 71 and R. L. Moore.

The map of Dovedale, based upon the Ordnance Survey mapping with the permission of The Controller of Her Majesty's Stationery Office ©Crown copyright 399531, has been drawn by D. G. Mackay.

Printed in Great Britain.
ISBN 0 85100 095 9